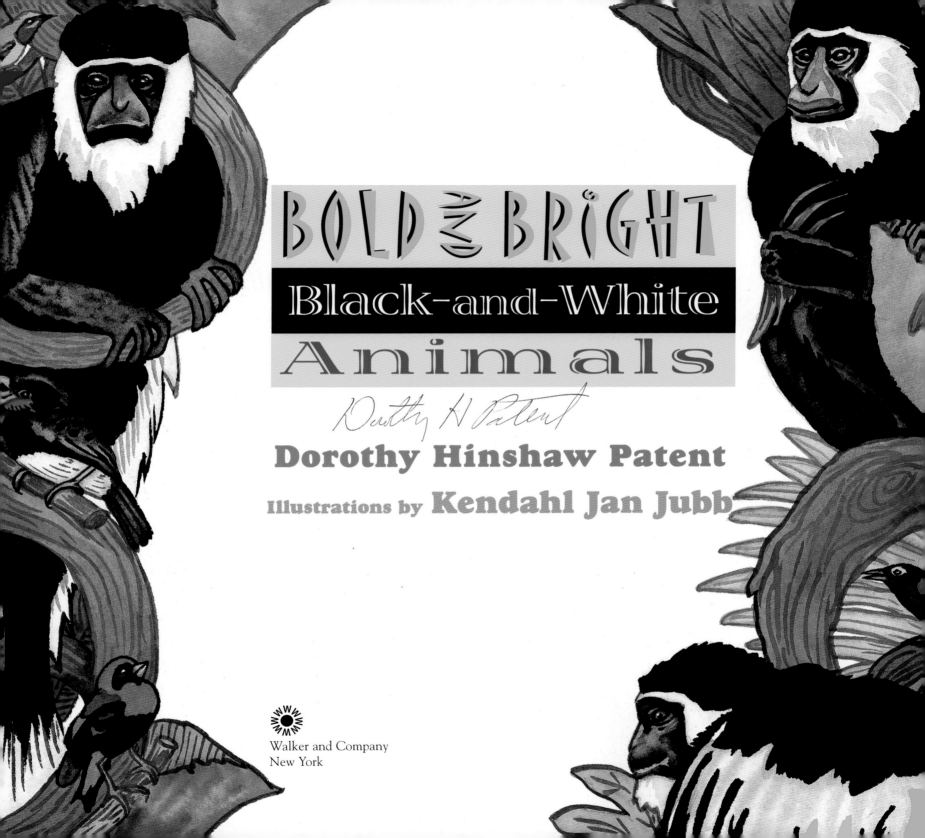

BOLD AND BRIGHT
Black-and-White
Animals

Dorothy Hinshaw Patent

Illustrations by Kendahl Jan Jubb

Walker and Company
New York

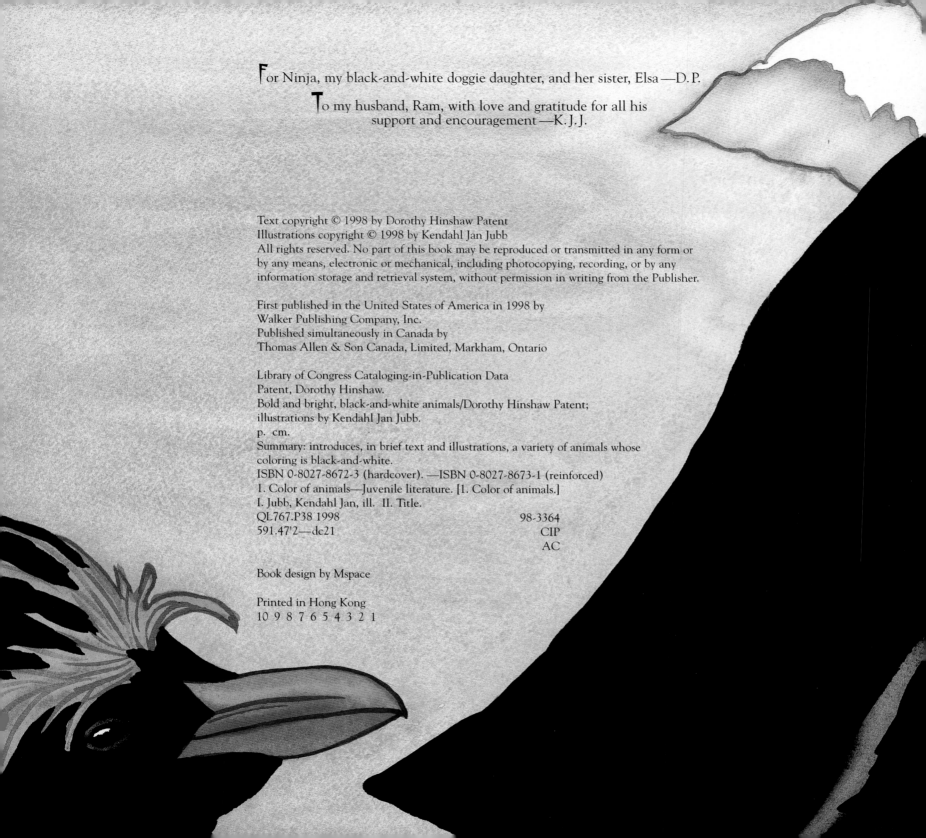

For Ninja, my black-and-white doggie daughter, and her sister, Elsa —D.P.

To my husband, Ram, with love and gratitude for all his
support and encouragement—K.J.J.

First published in the United States of America in 1998 by
Walker Publishing Company, Inc.
Published simultaneously in Canada by
Thomas Allen & Son Canada, Limited, Markham, Ontario

Library of Congress Cataloging-in-Publication Data
Patent, Dorothy Hinshaw.
Bold and bright, black-and-white animals/Dorothy Hinshaw Patent;
illustrations by Kendahl Jan Jubb.
p. cm.
Summary: introduces, in brief text and illustrations, a variety of animals whose
coloring is black-and-white.
ISBN 0-8027-8672-3 (hardcover). —ISBN 0-8027-8673-1 (reinforced)
1. Color of animals—Juvenile literature. [1. Color of animals.]
I. Jubb, Kendahl Jan, ill. II. Title.
QL767.P38 1998
591.47'2—dc21   98-3364
                                                               CIP
                                                               AC

Book design by Mspace

Printed in Hong Kong
10 9 8 7 6 5 4 3 2 1

Why are so many animals black-and-white?
Sometimes we know, sometimes we don't.
Even when scientists can't decide why an
animal is black-and-white, we delight in the
sight of this flashy color combo. So let's
take a look at some black-and-white
animals and see what we can learn
about them.

Striped Skunk

Day or night, no one can miss a skunk. Its white stripes stand out, even in darkness. Once you've smelled one, you know to stay away from *this* black-and-white creature. When that big, fluffy tail goes up, watch out! The skunk is warning, "If you bother me, *you'll* be sorry!"

Adelie Penguin

Black-and-white on ice—we can't help noticing a penguin. But in the sea, hunting for fish, it disappears. From above, its black back hides it in the dark water. From below, its white stomach and chest join with the bright light from above. But the camouflage doesn't always work.

7

Mountain Zebra

Stripes, stripes everywhere! It's hard to tell where one zebra ends and another begins. The stripes of zebras hide them in the dizzying herd. A hungry lion watching from the grass has a hard time picking out one animal to chase.

8

Killer Whale

A family of killer whales swims by, shiny
wet skin gleaming in black-and-white. Each
whale has a different pattern, so they can
recognize one another by sight. Being able
to tell each other apart easily is important in
a family. The whales know who is who even
from a distance, above the water or below.

Giant Panda

The panda is a mysterious animal.
Scientists once argued whether
it's more like a bear or a
raccoon. Now we know it
is more like a bear. But
the panda still has a
secret. No one knows
for sure why it is
black-and-white.
All we know is
that we love the
way this animal
looks.

African
Butterflies

Do these two African
butterflies look the same?
Not quite, but close
enough to fool a bird. The
right one tastes bad. Birds won't
eat it. The other one might be
delicious, but the birds will never
know because they leave it alone.

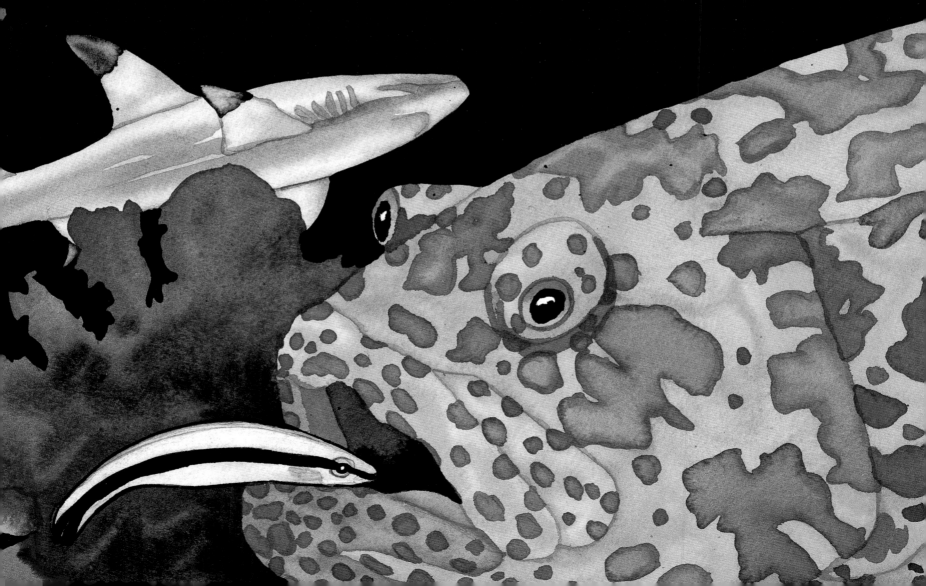

Sabre-Toothed
Blenny
and
Cleaner Wrasse

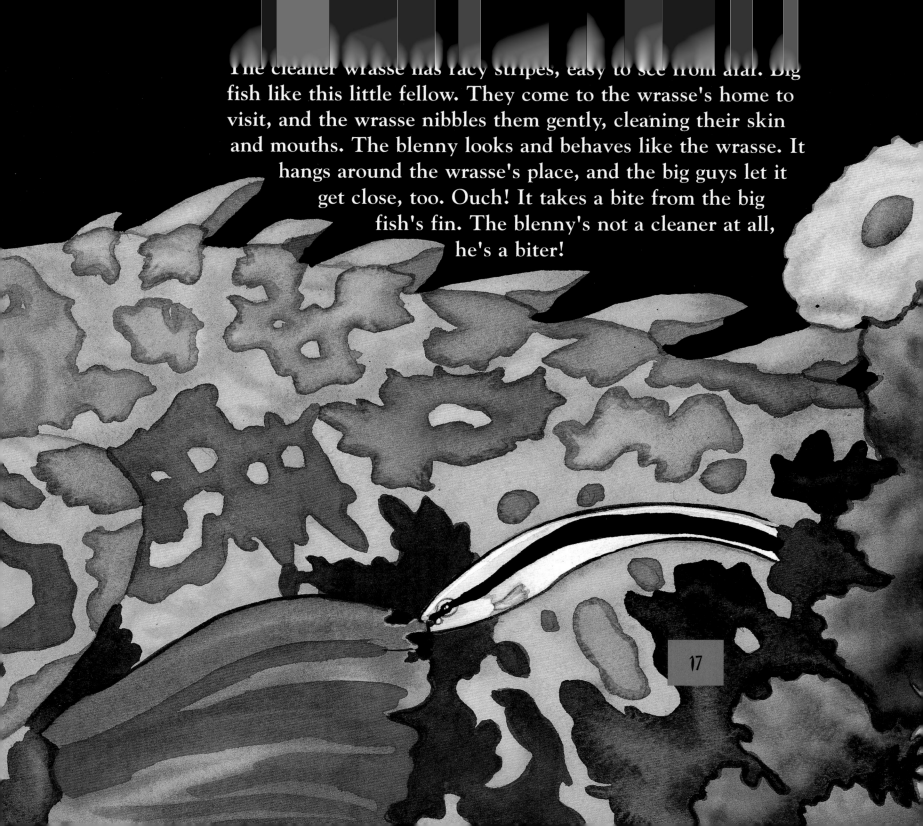

The cleaner wrasse has racy stripes, easy to see from afar. Big fish like this little fellow. They come to the wrasse's home to visit, and the wrasse nibbles them gently, cleaning their skin and mouths. The blenny looks and behaves like the wrasse. It hangs around the wrasse's place, and the big guys let it get close, too. Ouch! It takes a bite from the big fish's fin. The blenny's not a cleaner at all, he's a biter!

17

White Pelican

When a white pelican flies, you can see black feathers on the tips of its wings. The coloring material that makes them black also strengthens the feathers, and the wing tips need to be especially strong for flying in the wind. Other white birds, like snow geese and whooping cranes, also have black flight feathers.

Borneo Crab Spider

What is that blob on the leaf? Is it a bird dropping? The butterfly thinks so and is about to land there, seeking salt and moisture. But look closely—that's not a dropping at all! It's a hungry spider disguised with a bit of white silk, just waiting to make a meal of the butterfly.

Northern Pied Hornbill

You can't miss the huge beak of this black-and-white hornbill! It's useful for plucking fruit from trees. When it's time to nest, the female hornbill walls herself into a tree hole, where she and her young are safe. They count on the male to bring fruit and small animals to feed them through a tiny slit.

23

Sea Snake

In the water or on the beach, night or day, this black-and-white-banded sea snake stands out. What predator would want to eat something that could kill it with one poisonous bite? So the sea snake is free to hunt fish along rocky reefs and to come ashore to lay its eggs.

24

Ruffed Lemur

The black-and-white ruffed lemur, like all lemurs, lives on the island of Madagascar, off the East African coast. Its black face is surrounded by a thick ruff of longer white fur. Its long black tail helps the lemur balance as it leaps like a giant furry frog from tree to tree.

Marbled
Salamander

Carefully lift a log in a damp place and
you may be startled. If there's a shiny black
creature there, decorated with bands of white,
it's a marbled salamander. Its colors don't hide
it, they help a predator remember it. Any
predator that has gotten this salamander's bad
taste in its mouth once won't want to try again.

29

Domesticated Animals

Wild animals aren't the only ones with this attractive color pattern. People like it so much they have especially bred black-and-white animals such as the Dalmatian and border collie dogs, the Holstein cow, and the piebald paint horse. And even when they aren't a particular breed, black-and-white animals can be favorites, sharing our lives, at home and at work.

30

INDEX OF ANIMALS IN THIS BOOK

Adelie penguin—*Pygoscelis adeliae* 6–7

African butterflies—*Amaurus niavius* and *Papilio dardanus* 14–15

Borneo crab spider—unknown species 20–21

Cleaner wrasse—*Labroides dimidiatus* 16–17

Colobus monkey (guereza)—*Colobus guereza* 1

Giant panda—*Ailuropoda melanoleuca* 12–13

Killer whale—*Orcinus orca* 10–11

Macaroni penguin—*Eudyptes chrysolophus* 2–3

Marbled salamander—*Ambystoma opacum* 28–29

Mountain zebra—*Equus zebra* 8–9

Northern pied hornbill—*Anthracoceros malabaricus malibaricus* 22–23

Ruffed lemur—*Varecia variegata* 26–27

Sabre-toothed blenny—*Aspidontus taeniatus* 16–17

Sea snake—genus *Laticauda* 24–25

Snow goose—*Chen caerulescens* 18–19

Striped skunk—*Mephitis mephitis* 4–5

White pelican—*Pelecanus erythrorhynchos* 18–19

Whooping crane—*Grus americana* 18–19